Everything You Always Wanted to Know About Crop Circles*

*but were afraid to ask

By Lou Harry

BOOK PUBLISHERS

Kennebunkport, Maine

Everything You Always Wanted to Know About Crop Circles
Copyright © 2009 by Cider Mill Press Book Publishers, LLC
Concept © 2009 The Bob Staake Studio, Licensed by Synchronicity

All rights reserved under the Pan-American and International Copyright Conventions.

No part of this book may be reproduced in whole or in part, scanned, photocopied, recorded, distributed in any printed or electronic form, or reproduced in any manner whatsoever, or by any information storage and retrieval system now known or hereafter invented, without express written permission of the publisher, except in the case of brief quotations embodied in critical articles and reviews.

The scanning, uploading, and distribution of this book via the Internet or via any other means without permission of the publisher is illegal and punishable by law. Please support authors' rights, and do not participate in or encourage piracy of copyrighted materials.

13-Digit ISBN: 978-1-60433-061-8

This book may be ordered by mail from the publisher. Please include $2.50 for postage and handling.

Please support your local bookseller first!

Books published by Cider Mill Press Book Publishers are available at special discounts for bulk purchases in the United States by corporations, institutions, and other organizations. For more information, please contact the publisher.

Cider Mill Press Book Publishers
"Where good books are ready for press"
12 Port Farm Road
Kennebunkport, ME 04046

Visit us on the Web!
www.cidermillpress.com

Design by Megan Rotondo
Typography: Din, Bits Pics BT, and Washout
Printed in China

1 2 3 4 5 6 7 8 9 0
First Edition

Everything You Always Wanted to Know About Crop Circles*

*but were afraid to ask

Kit designed by Bob Staake
Book written by Lou Harry

Table of Contents

Disclaimer I	5
Disclaimer II	6
Introduction	7
In This Kit	8
About the Name of This Kit	10
Also Known As	12
New Word: *Cereology*	13
Another New Word: *Croppies*	13
Crop Circles: A Brief History	14
Circular Thinking	17
More on Flying Saucers	19
Hollywood Reinforcement	21
Signs: The Great Popularizer	23
The Grain People	24
Crop Circle Elements	26

The Mowing Devil	27
Holy Triangles!	28
Back in the Beginning	29
Peculiar Forms	30
Corporate Signs	39
Beyond the Fields	40
Naming Rights	40
Ancillary Effects	41
More About Colin Andrews	43
Meet Doug and Dave	44
Don't Let the Facts Get in the Way	46
Tools of the Trade	47
True Believers vs. Circle Makers	48
Crop Circle Tourism	48
Lines of Demarcation	49
Crop Circles and the Law	50
The End Is Near	51
Glastonbury Symposium	52
Great Moments in Crop Circle Pop Culture	52
Circle Soundtrack	53
Creating Your Own Crop Circle	54
Your Crop Circle: Defense	56
Essential Crop Circle Sites	57
In Conclusion	59

Dedication

This book is dedicated to William F. Nolan, Robert Silverberg, and all the other great science fiction writers whose novels and short story collections are boxed in my attic, waiting to be rediscovered. Thanks for the heads up about the future, guys.

Disclaimer I

If you have opened this kit in search of evidence that aliens have visited Earth, then pick up another book.

If you have opened this kit in search of evidence that magical forces are at work on the crops of the world, then you should also pick up another book.

Don't get me wrong. I'm not saying you should put this kit back on the bookshelf. Perish the thought. You've already opened the kit to find this book; the least you can do is pay its nominal ownership fee (and a bargain it is, don't you think?) and try to put it all back together.

Let me be very clear: what I am saying is that if you are looking to learn whether or not aliens have actually visited Earth, or whether or not crop circles have been created by some supernatural force, then you should get an *additional* book. This kit and something else.

That way, you'll have the satisfaction of having your alien and/or magical forces jones satisfied and, at the same time, proudly own this terrific kit.

Just so we understand each other.

Disclaimer II

On the other hand, let me disclaim this: if, attracted by the secret symbols that will rise from your crop circle tray, an alien spacecraft should choose to land on your desk ... or if an ancient druidic force is unleashed by your crop circle's latent power ... or if having greenery on your desk violates a company policy, and you find yourself having violated one company policy too many ... then you really shouldn't blame the creators of this kit.

You really shouldn't.

We're washing our hands of any responsibility for any of those possibilities.

We're all cool with that, right?

Right?

Introduction

Now that we've got those disclaimers out of the way, let me be the first to say "Congratulations."

Why?

Because you are now the owner of your very own crop circle.

Well, OK, not yet. But soon you will be.

Right now, you are the owner of all the elements to create your own crop circle. Which is a big step closer than you were before buying (or being gifted) this kit.

To fully realize how big a step this is, consider this: prior to your possession of this kit, creating your own crop circle would have required large-scale crop-flattening equipment, some willing accomplices, and cover of night.

That, or an extraterrestrial intelligence and/or ancient earth spirit who could guide you in the process.

Now, the times they've a'changed. In broad daylight (or, at least, under those headache-inducing lights in your office), you can now create a crop circle of your very own.

Just in case you've been interred, imprisoned, or in a coma for the past 30 years, I should probably explain that a crop circle is the common term for a massive geometric design that is pressed into the crops in a field. The stalks are bent down but not broken. And the designs aren't always circle-shaped, though the most basic ones usually are. As you'll read further in this book (or as you've noticed if you've already flipped through), crop circles come in many shapes, sizes and combinations. Calling them "crop circles" is really kind of trivializing.

Which doesn't mean I'm not going to do it. What else would you want me to call them? (More on what else crop circles are called later in the book.)

In this book, you'll not only learn how to make your own crop circle (which, to be honest, is relatively easy and could have been taught to you on an index card) but also learn about the history, lore, and speculation behind them. You'll be introduced to many of the most amazing crop circles on the planet. And you'll go along with me on many tangents, some of them actually related to the subject at hand.

Sure beats a desktop Zen garden, doesn't it?

In This Kit

No doubt you've already looked through the contents of this kit and tried to figure out what everything is. We'll pretend that didn't happen, though.

So here's a rundown of what you should have found when you opened this kit. You should become fully acquainted with all of the elements before attempting to grow your own crop circle.

- The first thing you probably noticed is the tray. Easy to spot. It's the biggest thing in the kit.
- Next up is the crop-growing mat. This is better than mere dirt. It's a scientifically advanced ultra-cool medium upon which to cultivate your seeds for optimal desktop growth.
- Then there's the grass seed. Without this key element, you've only got a plot of land. We would have gone with the traditional crop circle planting of wheat or barley, but it would take up far too much of your desk.
- Next in the kit is this book. If you find that the book is missing, then we've got a phenomenon more confounding than crop circles. For that means you are reading a book that you don't have in front of you. Try to wrap your mind around that.
- Last is your set of Crop Circle templates. You'll notice that one of these represents the face of an alien. Please do not take the inclusion of this adorable extraterrestrial to mean that the creators of this kit are endorsing the theory that aliens are

responsible for crop circles. In fact, we are remaining steadfast in avoiding committing to any theory.

Now, as to procedure, I strongly recommend reading the book before attempting to create your own crop circle. You can probably do it. You seem to be a fairly bright person. But there's information in here that might make the experience more satisfying.

If you absolutely insist on skipping ahead, though, and getting right down to planting, you can find the how-to section on page 55.

About the Name of This Kit

The kit that this book is part of has three words in its name. In the interest of clarity, let's take them one at a time.

MY: Let me make very clear from the beginning that when this book refers to *My* Crop Circle, it is actually referring to *Your* Crop Circle.

This by no means implies that when *you* refer to *My* Crop Circle that you are referring to anything but *Your* Crop Circle. You bought it. It's yours. Touch black, no trade backs.

Are we clear on that? Because I don't want a little pronoun trouble to ruin this for anyone.

Next word ...

CROP: In most cases, a crop is something that one would harvest. But if you harvest the grass seed you grow in this kit, you will have—no need to mince words—some shaved grass and a ruined kit.

For the purposes of this project, we mean "crop" in a more casual sense of the word. We fully realize that you wouldn't have picked up this kit if we called it My Grass Circle.

Although that might have gotten us reviewed in *High Times* magazine.

Final word. Here it comes.

CIRCLE: I could get snarky here and tell you that crop circles are called crop circles because if they were another shape they would be called *crop triangles* or *crop squares* or *crop parallelograms*.

But I won't get snarky.

Instead, I'll point out that the traditional shape of the crop circle is the circle because that is the traditional shape of the flying saucer.

More on the flying saucer later.

The reality, though, is that few crop circles consist of mere circles. Their designs have gotten more intricate over the past few decades. Show me a simple, circular crop circle, and I'll show you a farmer who doesn't even bother reporting it.

So there you go. *My. Crop. Circle.*

Also Known As

In this book, we keep calling examples of this phenomenon "crop circles."

But as the patterns grew in complexity, those words didn't seem to cover enough territory. And so the patterns were referred to (by those who regularly discuss such things) as *pictograms*, *agriglyphs*, or just plain *glyphs*.

These are not to be confused with the Guelphs, one of two warring factions that kept Italy lively during the Middle Ages. (The other gang were the Ghibellines, for the record.)

And Guelphs aren't to be confused with gorp, the yummy trail mix favored by scouts and comprised of nuts, dried fruit and, occasionally, chocolate (although, really, isn't chocolate in violation of the whole healthy snack thing?).

But you know what? It might just be easier to keep calling them "crop circles." So that's what

A Guelph who likes gorp.

I'll do. And I hope purists will forgive me.

New Word: *Cereology*

If people are going to study a phenomenon, then it's just a matter of time before that field of study gets a name.

Astronomers study the stars. Mathematicians study numbers. Someone who studies crop circles and their like is a *cereologist*.

Which, I realize, runs the risk that practitioners in this area will be forever confused with people who study Cap'n Crunch and the Trix rabbit.

Another New Word: *Croppies*

There are a number of historical uses for the word "croppie." It's been used to refer to someone with shortly cropped hair, particularly in France circa 1800. Around the same time, it was a nickname given to Irish rebels.

For our purposes, though, *croppie* refers to a crop circle enthusiast.

Now, if there were crew-cut French-Irish crop circle enthusiasts around the end of the eighteenth century, that would really be confusing.

Crop Circles: A Brief History

As ancient and mysterious as these shapes may seem, they are a relatively new phenomenon. It's not like Stonehenge, for

A croppie — the Irish kind, not the French or crop-circle kind

instance, which has been baffling humans for over 3,000 years.

Crop circles have, for the most part, only been landing attention for about 30 years. That's a two-decimal-point difference—kind of like the difference between being a millionaire and being a tens-of-thousandsaire.

OK, so there are some much older, crop-circle-ish things such as The Mowing Devil. I'll get to him a little later.

For the most part, though, the world started paying attention to crop circles around 1980, the same year that the U.S. boycotted the Summer Olympics,

Mount St. Helens erupted, and "Who Shot J.R.?" was a national question. It's also the year Christina Aguilera, Yao Ming, and Jake Gyllenhaal were born. Seems like only yesterday, doesn't it?

A simple crop circle

Into this world of 1980 came the concept of the crop circle. Baffling in their enigmatic simplicity, these awe-inspiring creations were nothing but 10-to-30-foot circles, concentrated primarily in England.

Here, for the record, is a short list of other things that are concentrated in England:
- toffee
- wickets
- places that end in –shire
- bangers
- mash
- dudes named Nigel

Pretty impressive, huh?

OK, maybe not. But crop circles are. They appear seemingly out of nowhere, under cover of darkness.

In addition to their mere existence, the patterns

were remarkable because the grain stalks were bent, not broken. The grains themselves were sometimes all bent in one direction; other times they were spiraled.

While at first the patterns were simple, things changed pretty quickly. Later, some of them became mind-bogglingly complex. (About now, you might be feeling an unexplained hankering to hit the Internet and do some searching for pictures of crop circles on your own. Go ahead, give in. It's easy. Try it. Some links are included at the end of this book.)

Not only did the designs become more complex as the years marched on, but the locations also spread to spots around the globe. Crop circles popped up as far away as Canada, Australia, India, and Japan.

Some were clearly the work of human beings—even the most hard-core

🌀 *A few mind-bogglingly* 🌀
complex crop circles

paranormalists were willing to admit that. For these do-it-yourselfers, crop circles set some dramatic challenges. Not only was there the challenge of being geometrically sound, there's was also the challenge of doing it at night, without anyone else knowing about it. Imagine Michelangelo trying to paint the Sistine Chapel without anyone knowing it.

Researchers bent on establishing a supernatural or paranormal explanation worked diligently to try to sort the hoaxers and crop-circles-as-anonymous-art folks from the rest (assuming the existence of a "rest").

And as the shapes become more complex, the more they suggested symbols of ancient cultures.

And that's when things started to get weird.

Circular Thinking

The big question most people ask when considering the crop circle phenomenon is: who or what is responsible? And while we know the source of some, there are a number of theories as to the cause of the rest. These include:

Aliens Among Us This theory posits that visitors from outer space haven't figured out how to keep their ultra-sophisticated vehicles from torching the ground beneath them. Somehow these extraterrestrials find value in making art of or pressing messages into remote fields. The movie *Signs*, which I'll get to in a bit, helped perpetuate this idea.

Nature According to this view, these shapes just, you know, happen. Like the face of the monkey in that picture of the moon, or the way that one peninsula on Lake Superior looks like a Sleeping Giant (at least that's what folks promoting Canadian tourism would have us believe). This theory was a lot easier to buy in early crop circle days, when simple, round shapes were the norm.

Another natural explanation has to do with the earth-flattening effects of ball lighting.

Weapons Could crop circles (or at least the ones that aren't hoaxes) be the aftereffects of weapons testing? Some think so.

Mystical Somethingorothers The epicenter of the crop circle world is England, where the phenomenon first gained worldwide attention in the 1980s. England is, of course, the land of King Arthur, Stonehenge, and the Magical Mystery Tour. Who knows what forces are at work in the English ether?

Once you buy into the world of magic, just about anything becomes possible. And any far-fetched explanation becomes fairly impossible to disprove.

Man-made/woman-made (Or, if the woman works as a domestic servant, then *maid-made*.) The idea here? A person deliberately and with forethought heads out into a field and carves out a shape in, one supposes, an effort to lead people to believe that the cause is actually the first item listed above. It is well established that many crop circles are created by people. Corporations have commissioned them. Some crop circle artists even go so far as to sign them. The question is whether these folks are responsible for *all* circles.

More on Flying Saucers

Didn't want you to have too wait too long, so here's what I promised earlier.

The flying saucer has been a part of popular mythology since the term was coined in the 1940s. Why the saucer? Credit a guy named Kenneth Arnold. Arnold was a pilot who, in 1947, made what is considered to be the first UFO sighting in the United States.

UFOs—technically, "unidentified flying objects (which actually means just about any object in the sky that you can't identify)—have been seen since people started looking up. One could say that the Bible is filled with them. There's the "thick darkness" spotted in Deuteronomy, the "chariots like a whirlwind" in Isaiah, the "continuing whirlwind" in Jeremiah, and Ezekiel's "great cloud" with "a fire infolding itself" and a "brightness about it." And plenty more if you're inclined to look.

Such sightings aren't limited to the ancient world. Check out the sky in the 15th-century painting of Madonna and child by Domenico Ghirlandaio. Look into the metallic thing that hovered over Chile in 1868. Or the 1909 buzzing of New Zealand. Looking back, you'd think we needed air traffic controllers long before airplanes were built.

Despite all this aerial activity, it was Kenneth Arnold's report that solidified interest in flying saucers. The short version of what happened is that Arnold spotted nine of the things as he flew near Mount Rainier in Washington while searching for a downed Marine Corps transport plane. He estimated that these objects, which he could not identify, were flying at 1,700 miles per hour.

In other words, they were flying really, really fast.

"A mirage," claimed the U.S. Air Force, but when the story got out and newspapers referred to Arnold's little friends as "flying saucers," the term stuck.

And soon flying saucers were being reported all

over the place.

Now you can consider the cause-and-effect of this two ways. You can choose to believe that what Arnold saw that day were, in fact, saucer-shaped extraterrestrial ships. If you believe that, then it stands to reason that there would be additional sightings. Someone had to be first, right?

Or you can believe that what Arnold saw weren't spaceships, but that his description lodged in the public consciousness so that anything unusual in the sky became labeled a "flying saucer." To heck with probability and proof; a flying saucer is a lot more interesting than a strange, unexplained light.

Whatever the case, the saucers had some help in the public relations department ... thanks to Hollywood.

Hollywood Reinforcement

Even with Arnold's report, "flying saucers" may well have disappeared from the public consciousness if it weren't for the powers that be in Hollywood. With Cold War concerns everywhere, studios found enormous story value in tales about what was going on "out there" ... and about what would happen if residents of "there" came here and disrupted our

American way of life and/or tested our military resolve.

And so 1950s movie screens were blanketed with the likes of *The Day the Earth Stood Still*, *This Island Earth*, *It Came from Outer Space*, and, of course, *Earth vs. the Flying Saucers*.

Some of these movies, by the way, hold up pretty well. I'm a big fan of the aforementioned *The Day the Earth Stood Still*—the original one, directed by Robert Wise, he of *West Side Story* and *The Sound of Music* fame. (Kind of makes you wonder what *Day* would have been like as a musical, doesn't it?)

Also holding up well are the suspenseful *The Thing* (very different from the gory remake) and *Them*, a film about giant ants—which isn't really an extraterrestrial film but I'm including it anyway because, well, who's going to stop me?

Anyhow, of our outer-space visitors, some came in peace. Some came looking for trouble. Some had unexplained motives. But while the good guys usually sent them back to where they came from, these creatures and their ships did have an impact on the real world: their existence on celluloid only encouraged additional sightings. Or provoked more aliens to visit Earth, depending on what or whom you believe.

Now, in those films not much attention is given to

what happens to the particular unlucky patch of the Earth upon which the flying saucer/alien spacecraft lands. Most of those movies focus more on how to deal with the creatures from beyond who were *inside* said spacecraft, and who are bent on taking over the world.

Such problems, as you can well understand, take precedence.

But one film did explore the connection between extraterrestrial spacecrafts and flattened farmland. And by prominently featuring crop circles in its posters and previews, it solidified the perceived link between aliens and crop circles. That movie was 2002's *Signs*.

Signs: The Great Popularizer

Hard to believe we're this far into the book without significant attention being paid to *Signs*. You really have to admire the restraint of the author, don't you?

OK, maybe you don't.

Written and directed by M. Night Shyamalan (a name that is a lot more fun to say than "Frank Capra" or "John Ford"), *Signs* arrived in theaters at a time when people still liked M. Night Shyamalan movies. It's about a former priest whose crops are circled. He's not alone. Crop circles are appearing around the world, and soon it's clear that they are linked to an alien invasion.

What Peter Paul & Mary and The Byrds were to the music of Bob Dylan, *Signs* was to crop circles. What I mean is, *Signs* popularized what was already out there among those in the know. Taking a concept familiar to conspiracy theorists and UFO buffs—on the order of swamp gas—it turned the crop circle idea into an everyone-has-heard-of-it pop culture touchstone. The hit film made the moviegoing public (which, roughly translated, means everybody and his brother) aware of the phenomenon and its suggested link to alien visitations.

And it didn't hurt Joaquin Phoenix's career, either.

I won't go into details about the plot of *Signs*. If you somehow have missed it, just put it in your Netflix queue and prepare for a fun night, especially if you turn your lights off and shut off your cell phone.

What's important here is that *Signs* was a hit. And like the flying saucer films of the 1950s, *Signs* penetrated public consciousness, creating a indelible image—much like a crop circle itself.

After *Signs*, it was difficult to see a crop circle and not think about aliens.

But enough about movies. Let's get back to the real thing.

The Grain People

While crop circles have appeared in a wide variety of fields, the easiest-to-work-with choices seem to be oil-seed rape, barley, and wheat.

Why? Because of the way these are grown and harvested. Experts say it's the smooth way the stalks overlap. A few words about each of these grains:

Oil-seed rape Call it rapeseed, if you want. Or, if you are as uncomfortable with the keyword as I am, just refer to it as rapa. Whatever you call it, this cousin of cabbage usually flowers bright yellow. In addition to its uses as a canvas for crop circles, it's most often used for vegetable oil and animal feed. You may know rapeseed oil by its more politically correct name, canola oil.

Barley Another basis for animal feed, barley is also a key ingredient in the creation of whiskey and beer. And it's also high in fiber and helps reduce cholesterol. Hooray for barley.

Wheat Do I really need to tell you about wheat? When it's not being pressed by crop circle makers, it's being turned into flour or pasta. Or shredded, squared, and topped with a nice sprinkling of sugar for breakfast consumption. Fun wheat fact: It's the number-one food item in the U.S., with per capita consumption exceeding that of all other staple foods.

That's the canvas. Now, about the designs.

Crop Circle Elements

Well, there's the circle, of course. And there's the triangle. Some crop circles are presented in spirals. Some have "key" elements—a line with a series of perpendicular extensions, like an old-fashioned key. The crescent is a popular shape. As are the star and the Celtic cross. There have been helix-shaped crop circles. And ones that seem to be outer-space maps.

Then there's the pictogram—which basically means that ideas are presented through pictures. In other words, these are crop circles with a message, whether literal, geometric, algebraic, or something else. There are many featuring complex symmetry.

And that's just the start.

But before we go further, let's drop back and take a look at some great moments in crop circle history, starting with ...

The Mowing Devil

Buffs point to this folktale as the oldest recorded incident, although they conveniently ignore the fact that it's clearly a tale. This English woodcut tells of a farmer who wouldn't pay for mowing, saying he'd rather the devil do it.

This is long before comedian Flip Wilson coined the phrase "the devil made me do it" in the 1960s. In fact, it was closer to 1678.

Anyone who has seen an episode of *The Twilight Zone* can guess what happens.

According to the not-particularly-well-developed story, the farmer soon discovered his field in flames. When the fires died down, the field was mowed.

The devil had, according to the narrator, "cut them in round circles, and plac't every straw with the exactness that it would have taken up above an age for any man to perform what he did that night: and the man that owns them is as yet afraid to remove them."

Frankly, I get confused after the "exactness" part. Admit it. So do you.

The story probably wouldn't have lasted so long if it didn't come complete with a groovy illustration of a devil making a large oval in the crops with a scythe. You'll see it in just about every book and on just about every Web site you find on the subject. I'm assuming the illustrator didn't acquire a copyright for it, or he'd be sitting pretty right about now.

The first known crop circle?

Holy Triangles!

Why do crop circles—at least, many of the early ones—seem so pure in their design? Croppies argue that their designs are based on sacred geometry— the same sort of patterns that have gone into the designing of altars and temples. The belief goes that sacred geometry taps into the basic patterns of the universe, and that studying these help gain insight into how the world works.

The circle represents oneness, for instance. And the point in the middle of the circle stands for the infinite.

Another crop circle shape is the "Vesica Piscis," which translates as "fish bladder" but in this case relates to the shape made by intersecting circles.

And don't get me started on triangles. There's something called the "golden ratio," involving ratios of sides in triangles that link future generations to our ancestors in ways that will make your head spin and your calculator explode.

Back to the Beginning

The father of crop circle reportage?

If anyone actually wanted to label someone in that way, the labelee would probably be amateur scientist John Rand Capron. One of the earliest references to crop circles comes from an 1880 issue of the journal *Nature*, in which Capron noted "a field of standing wheat considerably knocked about, not as an entirety, but in patches forming, as viewed from a distance, circular spots."

He went on to note, "I could not trace locally any

circumstances accounting for the peculiar forms."

Peculiar Forms

Speaking of peculiar forms, here's a range of them:

The Barbury Castle Appearing in 1991 near Wilshire, England, this set of interconnected circles and triangles is considered a benchmark in crop circle development. Geography nuts went crazy finding meaning in its angles. History buffs drew parallels to the 1654 book *Cabala in Alchymia*. Others just said, "Cool!"

The Stratford Eye No, it's not the name of a newspaper (although it would be a good one).

The Barbury Castle

And it's not a horror film ("Beware ... the Stratford Eye!").

In 1995, a crop circle later to be known as "The Stratford Eye" appeared near Stratford-upon-Avon (yes, the place your English professor went on vacation). While many saw this as the hallmark of authenticity, others noted that it bore a striking resemblance to the logo for the band Pitch Shifter, which was playing at a nearby music festival. Said one Internet poster: "It's mad, it's all gone mad. It's either that aliens like loud music or Pitch Shifter fans really like big graffiti."

The Stratford Eye — or an ad for Pitch Shifter?

The Julia Set Geometry students know a Julia set as a pattern involving fractals and other things I don't understand. To the rest of us, this particular Julia set looks kind of like a cocktail shrimp made from circular segments.

In 1996, a Julia set-shaped crop circle appeared and was noteworthy not just for its shape and

The Julia set—or a cocktail prawn? (Hey, that's what they call them in England.)

complexity, but also for its location: It was created just across the road from Stonehenge.

The site is even more mysterious because it was created very quickly, with pilots overhead not seeing the process and guards at the ancient neighbor site clueless about how the circle came to be.

Koch Snowflake

In 1997, near Silbury Hill, true believers and hoax-acceptors alike were impressed with a formation consisting, it seemed, of a six-pointed Star of David with each point turned into its own Star of David. Small circles surrounded each of these outer stars. Those who buy into numerology had a field day with all of the sixes.

This is one of a wave of crop circles related to the

The Koch Snowflake

science of chaos. I'll let the scientists figure out what that means. I—like, I'm guessing, most of you—have a limited understanding of chaos. And that understanding is limited to the understanding that when your desk gets too chaotic, you have to straighten it up before your boss gets pissed off.

Cambridge Bumper Crop The year 2001—specifically, the month of July, for whatever reason—was a big one for Cambridge, England. Not only did a major crop circle appear on the 11th, but it was followed by another on the 25th. Each appeared in opposing fields near Gog Magog Hills (a favorite of obscure-Biblical-reference scholars).

The first, nicknamed "The Big One," featured a 666-foot-wide outer circle that contained smaller formations, including a maze that at least one observer found challenging. The second formation, named "The Angel," was precisely the same size

The Big One and The Angel

as the other. This one, though, had a series of lines radiating from a halo-like inner ring.

Right Back Atcha Not all of 2001's activity was happening in Cambridge. Over near the Chilbolton radio telescope at Hampshire, a crop circle appeared that echoed a message sent to the stars back in 1974.

That original message contained some basic human information for the benefit of whatever or whomever would see it in the outer reaches of the galaxy. It include information on human DNA, the atomic table, and a kind of "You are here" map of our solar system.

If the crop circle

The original message sent out (in digital form—a string of 1s and 0s) to the great beyond. (left) The response? (right)

is to be taken at face value, it is a response to that note. It offers such adjustments as an added strand of DNA, a larger-headed humanoid, and changes to the solar system pic.

"Surely, aliens who can come to Hampshire are sophisticated enough to offer us more information than one can find on a fortune in a Chinese cookie," opined a report from the SETI Institute. (FYI: SETI stands for Search for Extraterrestrial Intelligence, and it's a respected, legit agency that concerns itself with life in the universe.)

The Milk Hill Galaxy Said to be the largest crop circle up to that point (August of 2001), a pinwheel design at Milk Hill, Wiltshire, measured 900 feet in diameter, and was comprised of 409 circles. What makes it even more amazing is the fact that it appeared after a rainstorm.

The fiction film *A Place to Stay*, a "tale of fate and human capacity for endurance in an uncaring world," included shots within this formation. Don't

The Milk Hill Galaxy
(If you rent A Place to Stay, you can see it move.)

worry if you haven't heard of the movie—it didn't get much of a release. (Need a review? Well, noted crop circle videographer Peter Sorensen called *A Place to Stay* "Superb!" and noted that it " ... simply and beautifully conveys the wonder and magic and the experience of being inside these magnificent temples of grain.")

You Want an Alien? We'll Give You an Alien

In the summer of 2002, a circle appeared in Hampshire featuring an impossible-to-miss image of an alien holding some sort of round, coded object. The creature looks like other images of our outer-space friends/enemies: elongated eyes, bald head, long neck, and a serious expression.

Some croppies were not impressed. Said Paul Vigay at www.cropcircleresearch.com, "It feels too Hollywood or *Star Trek* to my personal liking, which I don't think is indicative of the true circlemaking force."

By the way, Vigay also recounted a translation of the binary code on the

◉ *A self-portrait in grain?* ◉

alien's disc (some of which he checked himself). What did it say?

"Beware the bearers of false gifts and their broken promises. Much pain but still time. ... There is good out there. We oppose deception."

Sounds a little like a heartbroken woman at a bar in Hoboken, if you ask me. (Surprise: no one did.)

Wheat-out Any Clothes In March of 2006, Googlesightseeing.com reported on a crop circle in Sicily, Italy, that appears to be cut into the image of a nude woman (rear view). Since she is looking away, there's no way to identify whether or not this is meant to represent a specific woman or not.

Perhaps this points to a future where even crop circles will have to have parental advisory ratings.

🌀 Only in Italy, friends. Only in Italy. 🌀

The End of the World, 2006-Style

In 2006, a French military air traffic controller, Eric Julien, claimed that a comet would strike the Earth on May 25. He believed that our nuclear testing was endangering extraterrestrials—and they weren't happy about it one bit.

"I think that if we warn enough people living on the Atlantic coasts before May 25, 2006, the victims will be only 58 million. Otherwise, it will be worse."

Part of his evidence that major damage will be done? A crop circle that showed our solar system ... with Earth missing.

Yikes.

You may already know the outcome. At least, I hope you know the outcome. The Earth was fine after May 25, 2006.

Well, not exactly fine. But good enough.

You can relax now knowing, as you'll read in the next chapter, that at least some crop circles are in trustworthy hands ... those of big corporations.

What's missing from this picture?

Comin' at Ya

Also in 2006, a design appeared that has been called the first 3-D crop circle. In a wheat field in Oxfordshire, a pattern popped up that looks, from above, like a ground of skyscrapers emanating from a central sun. The work plays with perspective, with each of the "buildings" seeming to jut out toward the viewer—assuming the viewer is doing a flyby.

Aliens learn perspective.

Corporate Signs

There are some crop circles that are, without question, the product of humans. I'm talking about the plethora of corporate logos and for-hire efforts that have appeared on farmland.

The History Channel, for instance, hired a group to carve a circle with an embedded H. In 1998, Mitsubishi carved out a minivan in a field. A re-creation of the British Petroleum starburst appeared as a work-for-hire crop circle. And the logo for the Web browser Mozilla Firefox showed up in a Salem, Oregon, oat field in 2006.

Beyond the Fields

Like crop circles but not comfortable in a multi-season climate? Consider visiting—or making—snow circles or ice rings. These similar phenomena are rare, but have been spotted in the Himalayas and Sweden.

And cryptic shapes have been spotted in the sand near castles on seashores all around the world. But the origins of those are fairly clear.

Naming Rights

Half the fun of crop circles is the names assigned to them. Consider these colorful monikers given to actual crop circles:

The East Meon Pastry Cutter
The Torus Knot
The Beltane Wheel
The Snail

Insectogram
The Backhampton Triangle
Cheesefoot Head Punchbowl
Dancing Man
The Brain
Vesica Pisces
Meander
First Daisy
Beetlegram
Charm Bracelet
Hot Cross Bun
Solar/Lunar Crescent
Thoughts Bubble
Venus Fan
Cat's Cradle
Spinning Crescents
The Julia Set
The Barbara Castle Tetrahedron

Ancillary Effects

While there's no consistency in this, crop circles have been credited with a number of effects on the world around them. We don't guarantee that your very own My Crop Circle will cause any of this, of course, but its big brothers and sisters have been credited with all of the following:

Healing Show me a mysterious site anywhere around the world and I'll show you someone who claims that an ailment was alleviated. Freddy Silva, at Cropcirclesecrets.com, insists that "Crop circles, or the information carried within them, may one day be used as a simple, effective, and inexpensive method of healing." (For the record, I still recommend eating right, exercising, and having regular checkups with a medical doctor. Call me old fashioned.)

Euphoria Visitors have noted an increased feeling of joy when in proximity to a crop circle. That's understandable, especially if you've driven, flown, or hiked hours to find one.

Body Vibrations Got the shakes? A rumbling in your belly? Could be the power of the circle. Of course, you might just be chilly. Or have indigestion.

Magnetism Do crop circles or their creators cause an increase in magnetic readings? Or are crop circles or their creators attracted to areas with increased magnetism? Chicken? Egg? Whatever the case, these locations are known for their charges—and scientists and pseudoscientists have been postulating connections for decades. I'm skeptical, but still I'm not sure if I'd approach one if I had a metal plate in my head.

And then there's the **Viagra Effect**.

Crop circle researcher Colin Andrews and others have noted spending time in crop circles ... well, read the title of this section and figure it out for yourself.

Andrews, for the record, claims the phenomenon is psychosomatic.

But, of course, you—or someone you love—will have to decide for yourself.

More About Colin Andrews

Arguably the father of crop circle boosters (not literally, despite the preceding section), Colin Andrews was a British Government engineer who penned such books as *Circular Evidence* and *Crop Circles: Signs of Contact*. He was also a consultant on the movie *Signs*, which we discussed earlier. What you won't find in Andrews's work, unfortunately, is information on how much crop circle consultants get paid. Not that you'd necessarily find that information interesting. I, on the other hand, certainly would, since you never know if being the author of *Everything You Always Wanted to Know About Crop Circles* will launch me onto the speaking/consulting circuit. One never knows.

For the record, Andrews has written that he regrets speculating publicly that crop circles might be extraterrestrial in origin. "I should have been somewhat more circumspect when presenting the odder theories," he said in *Crop Signs: Signs of Contact.*

Yet he goes on to say he believes that "there is an intelligence behind the creation of crop circles. ... The placement of these designs seem purposeful to me."

In June of 1989, determined to see for themselves what was going on, Andrews and some colleagues set up a vigil for eight nights near Hampshire. He claimed to pick up some strange sounds, but the fact remains that no crop circles were witnessed in the making. The Committee for Skeptical Inquiry notes that nearly a hundred were created that summer prior to the project, dubbed Operation White Crow, and another 170 after. And the day after the program ended, a crop circle appeared about 500 yards away.

If aliens are responsible, they've got a heck of a sense of humor.

Meet Doug and Dave

A big wet blanket was spread over the crop circle world in 1991 when Doug Bower and Dave Chorley, two gents from Earth (England, to be specific), came out and said that they had been making crop circles for a dozen years. And they'd been doing it with only wooden planks and string. (They even signed some of their work with a telltale double D.)

What at first was an effort to convince the gullible that aliens were among us became an obsession: The men claimed to have been responsible for hundreds of crop circles. And they aren't alone. Many have come forward—and even demonstrated on camera how their work is done.

"Just because it doesn't sit in a gallery doesn't mean it's not art," said Matthew Williams. He's the Brit who had been fined in 2000 for damaging crops, and who released a video showing the secrets behind crop circle creation. There's also the Discovery Channel special, *Crop Circles: Mysteries in the Fields*, in which a team from MIT was dispatched with the mandate of creating a glyph comparable to that of existing mysterious cases.

The result? "After building what we consider a damn good crop circle with almost perfectly straight lines and an interesting geometry, I find it hard to put any faith in tales of crop circle construction by aliens," participant Dominic Rizzo said. "I think they are a result of free time, boredom and a good sense of humor."

Don't Let the Facts Get in the Way

What's interesting here, as with many so-called paranormal phenomena, is that evidence of fakery often causes an *increase* in belief. The fact that these guys irrefutably showed that man could, in fact, create very elaborate crop circle patterns only reinforced the conviction of true believers that there was something supernatural or beyond Earth at work.

This is a constant source of frustration for the folks at the Committee for Skeptical Inquiry (CSI—formerly known as The Scientific Investigation of Claims of the Paranormal, or SICOP). One of the best places to get the facts on alleged healers, spoon benders, and doomsday proclaimers, CSI points to the escalation in occurrences, the increasingly elaborate nature of circle creations, and the manner in which the occurrences spread geographically as further evidence that these are hoaxes.

Of course, whenever a bunch of paranormal phenomena are disproved, the diehard paranormalist will dig up an unsolved case. "OK," this argument goes, "those 122 tarot readers may have been fakers, but that doesn't mean that *my* tarot reader is a charlatan."

And so it goes.

Tools of the Trade

It's pretty much universally accepted that at least *some* crop circles are created by human beings. But a person can't do it without some tools. Here's a basic checklist for every would-be crop circle creator:

1. Guts. Gotta have 'em.
2. Friends who aren't going to turn you in. Don't underestimate the importance of this. Remember: trespassing is against the law. So is pushing other people's stalks around.
3. String or surveyor's tape. Nobody likes a lopsided circle. Or something like that.
4. A board with rope connected to each short end. You'll need something to do the flattening.
5. A garden roller. Frankly, I've never had more than a 20 by 20 patch of lawn, so I don't spend much time in gardening stores. You'll have to figure out for yourself what this thing is and does.
6. Patience. Crop-circle making has been described as boring, boring work. Be prepared to have to stay focused on minutiae for long periods of time.

I'm not going to go into detail on how the work is actually done. For that, visit http://www.circlemakers.org/guide.html.

True Believers vs. Circle Makers

The true believers—those who believe that some crop circles are the result of a supernatural or otherworldly force—believe that crop circle makers are muddying up their reality.

The crop circle makers—and those who appreciate the field patterns purely for their aesthetic and artistic value—see the true believers as nutso cuckoos.

Both groups can often be found on crop circle tours.

Crop Circle Tourism

While few people are unlikely to visit *your* personal crop circle (apart from a few curious co-workers or jealous family members), the biggie-sized versions in England are a big part of British tourism. Field guides have been published. Tour groups organized. Even helicopter tours are available.

The official tourism site for England, www.visitbritain.us, embraces the circles, while remaining noncommittal about their origins. "Despite attempts to dismiss them all as the work of human artists," sayeth the site, "some believe the evidence points to a much stranger explanation." What that explanation is, the site doesn't say. It does note, however, that about 250 designs appear around the world every year, with Southern England as the core of activity.

One thing visitors find at most crop circle sights are lines connecting or near the patterns. What's the deal with those?

Lines of Demarcation

In photos of crop circles, you are likely to see straight lines either cutting into the design or running alongside them.

What gives?

Well, these are one of the major reasons why many suspect that human hands are involved. These lines are known as "tramlines," and they are the very practical work of farmers who need paths to get close enough to spray their crops. Some speculate that there are fewer crop circles in the U.S. because, stateside, more farmers use aircraft to spray plants—which means fewer tramlines, which means more difficulty for crop circle artists to get at their canvases.

Crop Circles and the Law

Before you consider creating a full-sized crop circle of your own, consider the case of Gábor Takács and Róbert Dallos (I didn't say for you to try to pronounce their names, just to consider their case).

The two Hungarian high school students freelanced a crop circle—a pretty basic one—about 40 miles from Budapest in 1992, then went on TV to show how they pulled off the hoax. Smiles all around? Not exactly. Then 17 years old, Takács and Dallos were the first people to be legally charged with creating a crop circle. They were also sued by the landowners.

The ruling? The students were responsible for damages they created, but not for the damages created by the thousands of gawkers who visited the site. In the end, the TV show picked up the tab.

Interesting side note: after the crop circle was discovered, UFO siting reports began to appear. One UFO-ologist even went so far as to claim that the site *had* to have been created by an extraterrestrial intelligence. Of course, once the truth came out, these folks were less vocal.

The End Is Near

I'm not just talking about the end of this book, which is just a few pages away. I'm also talking about the end of crop circles.

The nature of crop circles is that they tend to be created in mature crops. That means crops that are about to be harvested. As such, each crop circle, not matter how elaborate, has a finite lifespan. Like ice sculptures, they are created with the knowledge that they will not last. At the risk of getting too philosophical, I believe that's one of the reasons why we find them so fascinating.

Glastonbury Symposium

Want to join like-minded (or semi-like-minded) crop circle enthusiasts from around the world? If so, the best place to be is the annual Glastonbury Symposium, held in July. Warning: it's not just crop circles that are discussed here. The program embraces any number of alternative theories, about everything from UFO studies to dowsing.

Great Moments in Crop Circle Pop Culture

Crop circles don't exist in a vacuum. They're part of the interconnected cultural landscape, as demonstrated by these pop side-effects:
- "Crop Circles" by Insane Clown Posse
  In this delightful tune, our narrator at first takes a realistic approach to the phenomenon (*Aliens, cults, witches with lawn mowers, mind blowers/ Nobody knows what for sure*), only to later discover that the circles are talking to him.
- Legendary band Led Zeppelin put a crop circle on the cover of its 1991 boxed set. Comprised of circles, connectors, and fork-like extensions, it's one of the most famous formations: Alton Barnes at Wiltshire. And it's the one that rocks hardest.
- "Crop Circles" by Monster Magnet
  This band takes a different approach, using "crop circles" metaphorically. Or something. (What else to make of *Come to me, I'm your living*

crop circle, yeah?)
- *Scary Movie 3*
  In this rather lame movie spoof, the targets include *Signs*, which is mocked by having farmer Tom (Charlie Sheen) discover a crop circle in the shape of an arrow pointing to his house, along with the words "Attack here."
- Crop Sector Ale
  The brewmasters at Wizard Brewery in San Leandro, California, came up with this concoction using "authentic crop circle barley."

Circle Soundtrack

What better way to get in the crop circle mood than by filling your iPod with circular classics? Here are some essentials:
- "The Circle Game"
  Joni Mitchell wrote it. Tom Rush popularized it. And the seasons go round and round. So do the painted ponies.
- "Round Midnight"
  Thelonious Monk's jazz classic doesn't have any words, so there really isn't much I can say here.
- "You Spin Me Round (Like a Record)"

The infectious 1985 song has won many music buffs a one-hit-wonder bar bet quizzing fellow inebriants as to the band responsible. The answer: Dead or Alive.
- "I Get Around"
The Beach Boys' 1964 hit is one of the few songs in pop music history that starts with the chorus. (Think about it.)
- "Circle" by the Ink Dot Boy
- "The Circle" by Dot Rotten
This sounds like music an alien would listen to.
- "Turn! Turn! Turn!" by The Byrds
- "Stonehenge" by Spinal Tap
- "Circle" by Harry Chapin
This may be the best song on circles ever written, though it has nothing to do with crop circles.

Creating Your Own Crop Circle

Now that you are an expert on crop circles, it's time for the moment you've been waiting for: the chance to make a crop circle of your very own.

In this kit, you have everything you need ... except for a little patience. You'll have to supply that for

yourself.
1. Here's how it works. First, you're going to place the crop-growing mat into the tray. (*Crop-growing mat* is the technical term for it. Telling you more would require special security clearance, and we don't have the time to check on all of you.)
2. Moisten the crop-growing mat with some water. A handy spray bottle is, well, handy for doing this.
3. Liberally scatter some seeds onto the crop-growing mat. Or do so conservatively. Lord knows we don't want to get into politics here.

Note: Please try not to make a huge mess. If you do, we are not responsible. Please refer to Disclaimer II on page 6 if you're fuzzy on this.

4. Using the aforementioned handy spray bottle, spray the seeds and mat with water until all is thoroughly moist, at least once daily.
5. Wait.
6. Wait some more.
7. Within from three to seven days, depending on various conditions, you'll see some tiny sprouts appear. When these sprouts are between ¼-inch and ½-inch tall, it's time to apply your chosen design.
8. Carefully cut out the template using scissors or

an X-Acto knife. Note the use of the word *carefully*. "My First-Aid Suture Kit" is not included here and must be purchased separately.
9. Carefully place the template over your crop of tiny sprouts. To help hold it down, stack a few coins on the template in several places. Keep watering everything daily—template, coins, and all. Wait even more.
10. Once you've got a lush, dense crop of grass that's at least 2½ inches tall (more is OK), delicately remove the template. *Voilà!* Behold your very own crop circle! Sit back and enjoy. Keep it from drying out, and it will last for many weeks.

Your Crop Circle: Defense

With your own crop circles comes some responsibility.

First, you may have to deal with the media. The media are fascinated by crop circles, so don't be surprised if you find photographers and/or nosy reporters sneaking around your desk. While this is to be expected, it doesn't mean that you need to tolerate more-than-reasonable attention. If the news media are distracting you or your co-workers from your important jobs, then higher-ups need to be contacted. As long as you are on private property, you should feel secure in asking the press to leave and wait for your press conference.

Second, there is the chance that skeptics will come by your desk to take a look, and then attempt to discredit your crop circle. Humor these folks, for they have sad little lives.

Finally, there is an outside chance that an alien or earth spirit will visit your desk in the mistaken belief that your crop circle is one of their own. Take heart in this, for it means that you have done an exceptional job in creating your crop circle. Think about it: you've fooled the experts. Given how little we know about these supernatural forces, however, it would behoove you to be as kind as possible with these creatures. Approach with palms up, hum a happy tune, and take lots of pictures.

Essential Crop Circle Web Sites

The following Internet sites were used for research in putting together this book. You are encouraged to waste valuable work time checking them out.

www.circlemakers.org Designed and maintained by artist and filmmaker John Lundberg, the site focuses on the myth and history as well as the how-to of making crop circles.

www.cropcircleconnector.com This up-to-the-minute guide offers the latest in crop circle reports and offers links to a wealth of other sites and information.

www.lucypringle.co.uk A great source of crop circle information, this site probably has more photos of actual crop circles than you'll find anywhere else.

www.glastonburysymposium.co.uk Follow this link and you'll learn more about the biggest crop circle conference in the world. Founded in 1990 by Roland Pargeter, it has continued to grow under various leaders. Conference topics range from rational science to pseudoscience topics such as astrology and feng shui.

www.seti.org When you want to hear from legit scientists and researchers on life in the universe, this is the place to go.

Note: Since this is the Internet, some of these sites may disappear before this kit hits the stores. That's no mystery. It's just the way things work these days.

In Conclusion

So who or what is responsible for crop circles?

As someone who likes to take people at their word, I'm more confused now than ever. As for you, well, you're free to believe any, none, or all of the confident folks quoted below.

"My information about the crop circles is that they are created by what is generally called UFO activity. The UFOs come in the main from Mars and Venus, not from outside our solar system."

—Spokesperson for Share International, a "worldwide network of individuals and groups whose purpose is to make known the fact that Maitreya the World Teacher for the coming age and his group, the Masters of Wisdom, are now among us." Quoted at share-international.org.

" ... when looking for an explanation of weird things, we should never omit from our checklist the possibility that the phenomenon we are studying is a hoax."

—Robert Todd Carroll, *The Skeptic's Dictionary*

"The Ball-of-Light Particle Model predicts they are caused by a ball-of-light [*sic*], most likely from

Solar Ball Lightning rather than Terrestrial Ball Lightning, that lands in a field of crops and decays in a 'frizzle' decay mode. ... Basically, it is a ball-of-light [sic] sitting there spinning—emitting photons as it does—where the top hemisphere is spinning one way, and the bottom hemisphere is spinning the other way."

—www.grandunification.com

"For the full answer ... I believe we may have to look to areas of wider consciousness that can bypass normal thought. ... I believe we cannot dismiss the possibility of some external intelligence being involved in this phenomenon."

—Lucy Pringle, *Crop Circles: The Greatest Mystery of Modern Times*

"I made my first crop circle in 1991. My motive was to prove how easy they were to create, because I was convinced that all crop circles were man-made. It was the only explanation nobody seemed interested in testing."

—Matt Ridley, *Scientific American*

"Crop circles are Chuck Norris's way of telling the world that sometimes corn needs to lie the $#@$ down."

—Internet joke

"Perhaps the mystery here is not what makes the circles, but what would cause so many otherwise normal people in southern Britain to make strange circles in the middle of the night in a farm field."
—The Unmuseum

"Whatever the force or entity may be that is producing crop circles, it is not from the known world."
—Patrick Cooke, *Alien Seeker News*

"I believe crop circles are created by planetary elementals of the air called 'Sylphs.' Sylphs may also be called 'Wingmakers.'"
—Zuerrnnovahh-Starr Livingstone, at www.educate-yourself.org

"What I have learned during my 20 years researching crop circles is that interaction is occurring between a creative intelligence and the human mind."
—Colin Andrews, *Crop Circles: Signs of Contact*

"You know, I'm the one responsible for those crop circles in England."
—Jerry on *Seinfeld*

About the Kit Creator

Bob Staake is an award-winning illustrator, author and inventor. His clients include *The New Yorker*, *The Washington Post*, Cartoon Network, Random House, Scholastic Books, Klutz Press, McDonald's, Mattel Toys, Ralston Purina, and countless others.

About the Author

Lou Harry doesn't mow as often as he should. This gave him time to write or co-write such books as *Kid Culture*, *The High-Impact Infidelity Diet: A Novel*, *Creative Block*, *The Entourage Handbook*, and *The Complete Excuses Handbook*. As Voodoo Lou, he penned *The Office Voodoo Kit* and *The Love Voodoo Kit*.

He lives in Indiana with his wife and four kids, none of whom have had any experience with the supernatural. Yet.

Photo & Art Credits

Pages: 15, 16, 34 (right), 35, 36, 39 © Lucy Pringle
Pages: 12, 14, 28, 31, 32, 33, 34 (left), 37, 38,
   Illustrated by Megan Rotondo

About Cider Mill Press Book Publishers

Good ideas ripen with time. From seed to harvest, Cider Mill Press strives to bring fine reading, information, and entertainment together between the covers of its creatively crafted books. Our Cider Mill bears fruit twice a year, publishing a new crop of titles each spring and fall.

Visit us on the Web at www.cidermillpress.com
or write to us at
12 Port Farm Road
Kennebunkport, Maine 04046